Zen Experience

Zen Experience

A Western Approach

DOUGLAS HARDING

The Shollond Trust
London

The original cover of *On Having No Head*

Published by The Shollond Trust
87B Cazenove Road, London N16 6BB, England
www.headless.org
headexchange@gn.apc.org

The Shollond Trust is a UK charitable trust, reg. no. 1059551

ISBN 978-1-914316-43-2
Cover design: rangsgraphics.com
(Original cover design concept: Douglas Harding)
Interior design: Richard Lang

Preface

On Having No Head by Douglas Harding was published by the London Buddhist Society in 1961. It was subtitled '*a contribution to Zen in the West*'. In the 'Publisher's Foreword' the reader was informed that: "This booklet contains a brief account of a remarkable Zen experience. Now that there is much talk of Zen for the West, it is important as the record of an experience in the mind of a man who at the time had no knowledge of Zen Buddhism. Only in his search for an explanation did he stumble into this field, and find what he needed. These chapters will in due course form part of a larger book called *Zen Experience, a Western view*, or some such title, but in our opinion they should be made available to all interested with the least possible delay." That larger book was never published. However, after Harding died (2007) I found amongst his papers the chapters that form this 'booklet'. Though Harding intended them to follow on from the first three chapters of the original *On Having No Head,* they make sense without necessarily being attached to that work. We are happy to make them now available.

Harding understood Zen. He understood Zen because he enjoyed, firsthand, *the central experience* of Zen — the direct seeing of Who we really are. He knew Zen from the inside. Harding was also inspired by Zen. "What I then found in Zen was the fruit and crown of all my past spiritual life — confirmation, tremendous encouragement, and many new perspectives opening out. It was a real home-coming. The absorbing and joyful work of self-discovery — culminating in seeing What I actually was — which had dominated all my adult life, was suddenly given fresh point and put in a much wider frame. From then on, a new openness and satisfaction supervened."

A relationship flows both ways. Though Harding gained from his meeting with Zen, Zen gained from its encounter with Harding, for Harding then presented the essential experience of Zen in a way that made it accessible to Westerners, or indeed to anyone. He demystified Zen. I accompanied Harding to America in 1974. In

New York he gave a talk to a Buddhist group. A man in the audience asked Harding about the meaning of a particular Zen question or *koan*. The *koan* was: 'How do you swallow the west river in one gulp?' Without missing a beat Harding replied that, though there wasn't a west river nearby, the East River was just up the road. If the man were to stand by it looking upstream then he would see the river flowing into him — into his limitless 'single eye' or 'mouth'. Harding avoided what could have been an inconclusive discussion by inviting the man to *experience,* for himself, 'swallowing' the river. And it wouldn't even give him indigestion!

Reading these chapters you will discover plenty about Zen. Harding knew his subject. But the main subject of the book is not Zen. It is you. Who you really are. In another version of his Introduction (not the one published here) Harding wrote: "…true Zen cares nothing about Zen, but only about direct seeing into our own nature. What makes for that end, here and now, is Zen, even if it never met that word; what does not, is not our Zen, even if every T'ang master said it." As Harding used to say: Before seeing Who you are, you read the scriptures to see if *you* have got it right. After seeing Who you are, you read the scriptures to see if *they* have got it right!

In the early 1970s Harding developed his *experiments*—awareness exercises which guide our attention to our True Nature. Harding's experiments, his 'skilful means', are important because they actually 'transmit the Light'. They make available the *experience* of our True Nature. One of the experiments involves you pointing at where others see your face and observing what you see there. Or rather, what you see *here*. Original! Unconventional! Straight to the point! "A special transmission outside the Scriptures." I think Hui-neng, the Sixth Patriarch, (who was adamant that people should SEE their Original Face rather than just think about it) would have appreciated Harding's skill, his ability to show people *where* their True Nature is — where it is *physically* — so that they can enjoy it whenever they wish.

Richard Lang

Contents

If thou desirest peace of mind and true unity of purpose, thou must put all things behind thee, and look upon thyself.

Thomas A'Kempis

We naturally believe ourselves far more capable of reaching the centre of things than of embracing the circumference... And yet we need no less capaciy for attaining the Nothing than the All.

Pascal

A sage is concerned with what is inside him. He abandons the That and lays hold of the This.

Lao-Tzu

Behold, the Kingdom of God is within you.

St. Luke

Introduction

This is not another book about Japanese and Chinese Zen. Already there are excellent accounts of the subject by Christmas Humphreys, Alan Watts, and other writers who — unlike me — are qualified to describe objectively the background, history, methods, schools, and cultural ramifications of Zen Buddhism in the Far East, and its coming West. Above all, there are the dozen or so works, as spiritually penetrating as they are comprehensive and scholarly, of Dr. D.T. Suzuki, most of them published in this country by Rider and Co. My own debt to these books is very great; and I assume that my readers, too, are familiar with at least some of them.

My own purpose is rather a different one: namely, to approach Zen from the West, in a thoroughly Western give-and-take manner. This programme calls for some explanation.

If we ignore its merely fashionable and beat varieties, there are, basically, two kinds of Western Zen, and both of them are no doubt necessary to its future here. The first gets as near to Eastern Zen as possible. Its ideal aim is mastery of the Chinese and Japanese languages, several years of zazen or 'sitting meditation' in a Kyoto temple under a qualified Roshi, the experience there of satori duly confirmed by him, and return to this country to build up here a branch of the Japanese tradition, transmitting in due course the true Dharma to a succession of Western masters. According to this school — it bears some obvious resemblances to Roman Catholicism — there can be no really *Western* Zen, home-grown and drawing its nurture from our own cultural roots. A clean break must be made. For Zen (it is said), in all its subtlety and hidden depths, is quite foreign to us: therefore it can be understood only on its own terms, according to its own strict rules, on the spot — even then they may elude the seeker.

The other kind of Western Zen agrees that the task is exceedingly difficult, and that, even if all our energies are engaged for a lifetime, success is not guaranteed. And it accepts with gratitude and enthusiasm the work of all those devoted scholars, such as John Blofeld, Chang Chen-chi, Charles Luc, Sohaku Ogata, Nyogen Senzaki, and of course Daisetz Suzuki, who have in the past thirty years made the masters' teaching available in our own language. It finds this teaching indescribably refreshing and inspiring, because it brings out so clearly and promises to develop so fruitfully tendencies which are already alive here, though neglected. Its firm conviction is that Zen can be deeply understood by Westerners, and really lived here, *only* in a Western way, honestly and unashamedly, and it is no good our trying to turn ourselves into orientals. Even if we could deny and live down our entire past, our uniquely valuable heritage (and, thank God, we can't), we should only be denying Zen as well. For the spirit of Zen is profoundly sane and natural. It abhors the contrived and the remote, and is always pointing to the ordinary, the given, the here and the now. Our despised present circumstances, just as they are at this moment and with all their seeming obstacles to Enlightenment, are in fact precisely what is needed for that purpose, and all postponement to a more convenient date, all displacement to a more propitious spot, is nothing but escape from that Absolute Perfection which is nowhere but here — if only we could nerve ourselves to see it, and to trust what we saw.

Besides, Zen owes its special character, its very existence, to its immense self-confidence and indeed cocksureness, its terribly high-handed way with the hallowed tradition which it brought from the land of its origin. Indian Mahayana Buddhism, transplanted into the very different cultural climate of 5th and 6th-century China, and with Taoist shoots grafted on, soon became another kind of tree altogether: hence its astonishing vigour, sustained right up to recent times. And now, fourteen centuries later, a similar transplanting is in progress, with the possibility of equally fruitful though equally disconcerting results. The domestication of Zen here has begun, not only to awaken us to neglected sides of ourselves, but also to enliven

Zen itself. There are indeed grounds for believing that while Zen is slowly dying in the East, crushed under the weight of its own ossified traditions, it is being reborn here unencumbered. Having for us shed most of its accidental accretions of sanctity, formalism, prestige, social and political involvements, ritual, pious verbiage, and general stuffiness and squareness — not to say humbug — the wonderful Essence is free once more, as in the T'ang and the Sung, to shine forth in all its clarity and brilliance.

I need hardly point out that it is this second view of Western Zen which I am adopting here. That I have little choice in the matter, my own history shows. I knew almost nothing about Zen till I was getting on for fifty, and had already with diligence worked out my own salvation after my own fashion, in true Western individualistic style. What I then found in Zen was the fruit and crown of all my past spiritual life — confirmation, tremendous encouragement, and many new perspectives opening out. It was a real home-coming. The absorbing and joyful work of self-discovery — culminating in seeing What I actually was — which had dominated all my adult life, was suddenly given fresh point and put in a much wider frame. From then on, a new openness and satisfaction supervened.

I took to Zen at once, because I was already a Zen man. And this was surely no fluke, but part of a trend: while Zen is losing much of its relevance in the Far East (already it is dead in China) it is gaining relevance here, and in some ways becoming more at home in London and New York than in Tokyo. Of course the scion here is weak and tiny compared with the parent tree over there, but it is healthy and promising enough.

My present purpose is to promote this growth by giving some account of my own experience. It is the only thing I am fitted to expound, and contains all the help I could conceivably offer — by way of encouragement, stimulus, and perhaps warning — to others in search of themselves. And it is an essential part of my experience of Zen that (though its exquisite flavour, clarity, and charm are certainly unique) it unites intimately and at many points with our European genius — religious, philosophical, scientific, and even humorous — as well as with the Indian and Middle-Eastern. Sometimes, indeed, it fulfils our thought, and is more ourselves than we are. But all these divisions, once so real, are in the modern world becoming increasingly meaningless. To plump for either the East or the West, to prefer Zen or any other mystical school *on principle*, instead of taking from each what speaks to our condition, is to close mind and heart and to contradict the generous spirit of Zen itself. Even to label ourselves Zenists or Zen followers, here and now in the West, is really somewhat of an absurdity. For (as I shall show) it is vital to Zen that it shall be unprejudiced and free, spilling over in all directions and turning up in many unlikely places, from logical positivism to Alice, and from 3rd-century Gnosticism to the *Chasidim* of 19th-century Poland. In every sense, Zen is big; otherwise, it wouldn't be worth bothering about.

This book is anything but an objective exposition of Zen, presenting a balanced view from outside, for outsiders: if it were, these overspills into alien traditions would only confuse the issue. In fact, it is an earnest invitation to come right in, and therefore concerns itself only with the practical question of how to enter. I must assume that for the reader, as for myself, the only thing that matters is, somehow or other, to find out What we really are, to *see* into our true nature, breaking if need be all the rules and using any improvised tool that comes to hand. This is, or was, the sole purpose of Chinese and Japanese Zen. And whatever in Zen, or outside Zen, puts off that discovery, is all wrong. And so I have passed on all the hints, all the dodges and tips and pointers I know, on the off-chance of one or other of them working for the reader as they work for me, nudging us till we turn round and look in and see clearly Who is here. I can't help it if some of these expedients look deplorably unZen-like or profane or even frivolous. Genuine Zen never has been Zen-like, and predictable, and careful not to shock itself — what's the use of upsetting all conventions except one's own? Absolutely anything goes, if only it will bring us to that Vision.

The author cannot sufficiently acknowledge his debt to his son Julian (Ming Ching), to whom the book is lovingly dedicated.

There was a little city. And there came a great king against it, and beseiged it, and built great bulwarks against it. Now there was found in it a poor wise man, and he by his wisdom delivered the city; yet no man remembered that same poor man.

Ecclesiastes

> There is an inmost centre in us all,
> Where truth abides in fullness; and around,
> Wall upon wall, the gross flesh hems it in,
> This perfect, clear perception — which is truth.

Browning

A man has many skins in himself, covering the depths of his heart. Man knows so many things; he does not know himself. Why, thirty or forty skins or hides, just like an ox's or a bear's, so thick and hard, cover the soul. Go into your own ground and learn to know yourself there.

Eckhart

> There was a little green house,
> And in the little green house
> There was a little brown house,
> And in the little brown house
> There was a little yellow house,
> And in the little yellow house
> There was a little white house,
> And in the little white house
> There was a little heart.

Nursery Rhyme about a Walnut

Chapter 1

To The Centre

Ordinarily, my so-called waking life is a dream, a trance. My attention, absurdly detached from its source and centre here, is fastened upon the surrounding world, upon the phenomena of my periphery, as if these images were self-supporting and independent of me. I regard them as real, and myself as unreal. It is as though, incurably long-sighted, this observer could never bring himself into focus, but must always over-look his own existence here and now. We all suffer from this astonishing defect of vision: as I walk in the street, I note around me the preoccupied and absent faces intent upon the *other* faces, the clothes, the shop windows, the cars — intent upon anything and everything but the faceless one who is intent. We live off-centre, as if we had no centre. We cannot face ourselves.

It is desperately difficult to wake from this dream. Courage is needed, and great persistence. As the *Katha Upanisad* puts it: "God made sense turn outward: man therefore looks outward, not into himself. Now and again a daring soul, desiring immortality, has looked back and found himself."

To reverse this centrifugal tendency of mine, I have to break a life-long habit. Turning inwards, I must move against the outflowing stream and boldly make for its source. Everything short of this inmost well-spring and centre of mine, everything — no matter how excellent — which is peripheral, is to be passed by. "The true Buddha sits in the interior," says the Zen master Chao-chou T'sung-shen (778-897). "Bodhi and Nirvana, Suchness and Buddha-nature — all these are outer clothings, defilements... Ever since my interview with this old man, I am no other person than myself — I am master of myself. It does not profit you to seek this man in the outside world. When he is right here do not fail, by turning round and looking the 'wrong' way, to interview him."

LOOK IN! This vital turning round or true conversion, though variously described in different religious traditions, is insisted upon by all the great teachers. It is what the *Chandogya Upanisad* calls "finding your way back into yourself"; what the Taoist *Secret of the Golden Flower* calls "the backward flowing movement, looking inwards at the room of the ancestors"; what Plotinus calls "withdrawing into yourself and looking"; what the Zen master Neng of Yun-chu calls "throwing your light inwardly, to see by yourself what is this body of yours, this mind of yours"; what Kabir calls "entering into your own body." In fact, as Kabir points out, you discover there "neither body nor mind... You shall find naught in that emptiness. Be strong, and enter into your own body: for there your foothold is firm. Consider it well, O my heart! go not elsewhere. Kabir says: 'Put all imaginations away, and stand fast in that which you are.'"

It is true that those who have dared to turn round and gaze within do not always describe what they find as the Void, or Emptiness: it may appear rather as Light, or the true Self, or Pure Consciousness, or God. Thus St. Augustine: "Being admonished to return to myself, I entered even into the secret chamber of my soul... And I beheld with the eye of my soul the Light unchangeable." And Ramana Maharshi: "If the mind is turned in, towards the Source of illumination, objective knowledge ceases, and the Self alone shines as the Heart... We are to dive in to the Self." But what no serious seeker here has ever found is a head, or a body, or any thing. "In this kind of seeing," says *The Secret of the Golden Flower*, when the eye looks inwards, "one only sees that no shape is there." This is where nothing human or phenomenal can survive. In the splendid language of the *Mundaka Upanisad*: "As rivers lose name and shape in the sea, wise men lose name and shape in God, glittering beyond all distance."

* * * *

The soul has often been pictured by primitive peoples as a manikin living in the human head, and the same idea recurs in many Hindu and Taoist scriptures. The *Svetasvata Upanisad*, for instance, speaks of the Lord who lives "in the faces, the heads, the necks of all." The beautiful old Christian hymn which begins "God be in my head" echoes the same universal idea. Even Buddhist scriptures sometimes seem to say that this flesh has a divine Inhabitant. The *Diamond Sutra*, for example, describes the Tathagata-garbha as "hidden in the body of every being, like a gem of great value wrapped in a dirty garment."

This idea is well-founded on fact, on the most wonderful of facts: the spot I call HERE really is the holy of holies, God's inmost temple. But He is not in my head: He is *instead* of my head. My head has taken itself off, leaving the site clear of every obstruction. "God be in place of my head" would be a more sensible prayer, and one that is invariably granted. "God entered the body," says the *Aitareya Upanisad*, "and rejoiced to find there nothing but Himself." And indeed there is no room here for anyone else: my physique is crowded out, so to speak — pushed over there by this cuckoo-like Guest. In Eckhart's homely language: "God wants this temple cleared of everything but Himself. This is because this temple is so agreeable to Him and He is so comfortable in this temple when He is here alone." In any case this is His true address: man's is always next-door. As the *Koran* observes, God is nearer than one's own neck-vein. Tennyson's "Closer is He than breathing, and nearer than hands and feet" is an accurate statement and no mere metaphor. God does not inhabit my head, but rather this cavity, this "hole where a head should have been". "Brahman, the Truth, the Supreme, the only One," says Sankara, "is in the *cavern* between the eye-brows; whoever dwells in that Centre has no rebirth."

And it is not that, somehow or other, I can gain access to this divine Centre: I am here for good, and have access to nothing else

---

Cf. Lieh-tzu: "The Unborn is by our side yet alone."

Cf. *Katha Upanisad*: "The wise... discovering in the mouth of the cavern, deeper in the cavern, that Self, that ancient Self... pass beyond joy and sorrow."

whatever. In reality, the Taoist *Hui Ming Ching* has no need to urge me:

> Kindle Light in the blessed country ever close at hand,
> And, there hidden, let thy true self eternally dwell.

For I am that Light, and there is no other. The divine is this and here and now; the human is that and there and then. If what is always here or present truly exists, and what is always over there or absent does not, then St. Catherine of Siena's favourite dictum certainly applies: God is He who is; man is he who is not. Indeed it is His very nearness which hides Him. As Rumi observes:

> The Spirit thou canst not view, it comes so nigh.
> Drink of this Presence! Be not thou a jar
> Laden with water, and its lip stone-dry;
> Or as a horseman blindly borne afar,
> Who never sees the horse beneath his thigh.

My blindness to this Presence — my imagined absence or eccentricity — is curable: I have only to turn round and give the command LOOK WHO'S HERE! Then at last it is plain who and where I am. The Prodigal Son, coming in the end to himself, returns to the Father's House he had never really left; the lost Prince, having been brought up by pauper foster-parents, discovers his royal ancestry and claims his rightful throne; the poor boy is given some magical source of unlimited wealth and power.* Half the world's fairy tales tell this truest of all stories, the ultimate success story. We are all

---

*The Buddhist version of the Prodigal Son story, in *The Lotus of the Wonderful Law*, closely resembles that in the Gospel: except that the Father is able only by degrees to persuade his returned son that he is His heir and immensely rich. There is another Buddhist parable of a Prince who thought he was a pig, lived in a sty with a sow, and raised a large litter: again, he was not easily persuaded to change his mind.

infinitely rich and noble and fortunate, if only we knew it: for, as Hakuin points out in his *Song of Meditation*:

> Sentient beings are all primarily Buddhas...
> Not knowing how near the Truth is,
> People seek it far away — what a pity!
> They are like him who, in the midst of water,
> Cries out in thirst so imploringly;
> They are like the son of a rich man
> Who wandered away among the poor...
>
> For such as, looking within,
> Testify to the truth of Self-nature,
> To the truth that Self-nature is no nature...
> This very spot is the Lotus Paradise,
> This very body the Buddha.

As Hakuin says, when we look within at our Self-nature, we find it is no nature at all. I can discover here no Self, no I, no Consciousness, no Mind, no God, no Light, no Emptiness, no Void, no Substratum of any kind — not even Nothing. It is true I have used such terms, loosely and as figures of speech, to describe what it is like here, and I shall have to use them again. But strictly speaking, if I honestly take myself as I find myself, I fail to detect anything. Here and now there survives not the slightest trace of any person or thing or quality, not the faintest lingering scent or shadow or stain of them. And where am I if not here and now?

It is one of the merits of Buddhism that it has, more than other religions, refused to attribute to Reality any virtues or qualities at all, however abstract or basic. It follows the negative path of the mystics to the very end — if there were an end. This is because final release, the removal of every doubt and defilement and karmic effect, can only be had (as the *Itivuttaka*, a Pali scripture, puts it) "in the destruction of the substratum." The idea of Reality, as something specific and contrasted with Unreality, as something to hold on to, has to go. Plunging down and down into ourselves, we meet no obstruction whatever, no utmost limit or floor, nothing that can be thought about or named. We see that we are absolutely unconditioned: not merely free from the blemish of selfhood, but of being as distinct from non-being. "Even oneness itself remains not," says Seng-t'san (d. 606): it turns out to be yet another artificial, mind-made limitation, an impurity that has to be washed away.

Such obstructive reifications are always crystallising, and constant vigilance is needed to dissolve them. Hui-Neng, following the *Prajnaparamita* philosophy, was fond of saying that from the first, not a thing exists: our self-nature is absolutely pure and empty. Nevertheless a number of his followers made a something of this purity, and started looking in themselves for it, as if it were a separate entity from the one who is looking, an ethereal and transparent object of some kind. Again, the idea of the Void, or *sunyata*, which is basic in Mahayana Buddhism, is always tending to become an idea of something attainable, something to practise and make a habit of, something to treasure and get attached to, something to believe in and argue about and make a dogma of and use for purposes of self-affirmation: in short, it is always turning into its very opposite, and only resulting in more misery and bondage instead of release. And so the *Mahaprajnaparamita* has good reason to include, as the fourth of its eighteen varieties of emptiness, the emptiness of emptiness itself, the voidness of the very notion of voidness. Every support has to be thrown aside, every hold relaxed, every idea exploded, every possession given up, every point of reference lost, every retreat cut off, and indeed every abandonment abandoned. Only then are we stripped quite naked, and ready to take the final plunge into the abyss of our own nothingness. Only then, in other terms, are we simple and childlike enough to stop thinking and look at what we are. The scales of thought fall from our eyes: we are no longer blind to the obvious; we enjoy what Suzuki calls the simplest possible experience, "because it is the very foundation of all experiences." Not that the truly simple is either common or easy: as Suzuki points out, "It requires the highest degree of intellectual perspicuity to look into Reality in its suchness and not to weave around it subjectively-constructed meshes."

These meshes are all manner of protective devices and camouflage. We fear the emptiness which is our real nature, and will go to endless trouble to hide it from ourselves. It is as if this central abyss were not our precious life-source, but some dreadful gaping wound which must be bandaged and concealed at all costs. In fact, this cowardly refusal to acknowledge what we are is the cause of all our unhappiness. Conversely, in the words of the Tibetan master Gampopa, "It is great joy to realise that the Fundamental Reality is qualityless." When at last, plucking up our courage and turning round and steadfastly gazing upon ourselves, we see that we are transparent and void through and through, there is a wonderful feeling of relief. All our cares vanish in the pure and brilliant light of that Perfection, no dark spot remaining. "Into the soul's essence," says Eckhart, "no speck can ever fall."

In fact, the greatest and boldest of the Christian mystics, from Dionysius onwards, are as alive to the void as any Zen master. "Paul rose from the ground wide-eyed, beholding nothing," writes Eckhart. "He saw nothing, to wit, God... It appeared to one soul as in a dream (it was a waking dream), to be big with naught like a woman with child, and in this naught God was born, the fruits of the naught... He had a vision of God where there are no creatures. He beheld all creatures as naught for he had the whole essence of creatures in him. He is the all-containing essence." And this divine essence is described by Eckhart in another sermon as not-God, not-spirit, not-Person, not-image, but "sheer, pure limpid unity," in which we must "sink eternally from nothingness to nothingness."

Ruysbroeck goes almost as far. He writes of the illumined man: "In the deeps of his ground he knows and feels nothing, in soul or body, but a singular radiance with a sensible well-being and an all-pervading Savour. This is the way of emptiness." Elsewhere he describes the God-seeing man as one who feels that the foundation of his being is abysmal; whose inward exercise is wayless, bottomless, and measureless; and who dwells in a knowledge which is ignorance. Angelus Silesius is another who is not frightened to look within, and whose courage is infinitely rewarded:

> See, where thou nothing seest;
> go, where thou canst not go;
> Hear, where there is no sound;
> then where God speaks art thou.

Clear vision and enjoyment of the abyss are, however, far from typical of Christian piety. More often, sensible consolations are earnestly sought, warm devotional feelings of love and pity are cultivated, pious imagery evoked, acts of will practised. And when the contemplative, advancing beyond this stage, suffers dryness or poverty of thought and emotion, the result is likely to be deep anxiety or even despair: the half-glimpsed void is feared and resisted. But such experienced spiritual directors as de Caussade know that this seeming lack is really our treasure, and a most encouraging sign. Indeed this is the main theme of his letters. Concerning "voluntary annihilation" he writes to a nun: "The more we realise our nothingness the nearer we are to the truth... The understanding, the memory and the will are in a fearful void, in nothingness. Love this immense void... Love this nothingness since the infinitude of God is there." And he assures another religious that the great emptiness she suffers will lead to more spiritual progress in one month than years of sweetness and consolation could ever do.

The authentic seeing, according to the Zen masters, is seeing into this emptiness or nothingness, into the absolute Void of our true nature. All other seeing is mis-seeing, like taking a mirage to be an oasis. We smile at the crudity of Laplace's silly gibe that he had searched the heavens and found no God. In fact, he had the right idea: at least he didn't commit the fatal mistake of looking for God in some beautiful spiritual heaven dreamed up by the pious, as a refuge from this harsh world. The trouble was that he attended to what lay at one end of his telescope, and neglected the other. If only he had looked in both directions, into the starless Void within as well as the starry void without, he would have seen God more clearly than the brightest star: there is always perfect visibility at the astronomer's end of the telescope. Immanuel Kant knew better than this savant with a one-track mind: two things moved him to wonder — the starry vault above, and the soul within. And the Irish mystical poet A.E. knew better still:

> These myriad eyes that look on me are mine;
> Wandering beneath them I have found again
> The ancient ample moment, the divine,
> The God-root within men.
>
> For this, for this the lights innumerable
> As symbols shine that we the true light win:
> For every star and every deep they fill
> Are stars and deeps within.

These deeps are visible. "I see God more real than I see you," said Ramakrishna to Vivekananda. According to Meher Baba, another Indian master of our own times, the advanced aspirant "sees God directly and clearly as an ordinary person sees the different things of this world." Provided we have no fixed thoughts about it, says Seng-t'san, the Third Patriarch of Zen, we may see the Perfect Way before our very eyes. Here he speaks the universal language of the mystics, with its emphasis on sight: they are the Seers of the Real; gifted with clear vision, they are illumined or enlightened. Nor are these merely convenient metaphors. "Look, look!" exclaim the Zen masters, and the very last thing they mean is "Think, think!" You actually see your original face with your third or spiritual eye, says Herrigel: you don't invent it. Seeing it to be here is quite a different thing from knowing it to be here. The Buddhist way of indicating "the immediacy and utmost perspicuity and certainty" of what is experienced at the moment of enlightenment, Suzuki points out, is to describe it as seen, or seen face to face. "Thus knowing, thus seeing" is a set phrase in Theravada as well as Mahayana literature, implying that knowing which is not also seeing may well be mere knowing about.

The sage Ramakrishna did not exaggerate: the Self or God really is more visible than any man. Paradoxically, it is because He is Nothing to look at that He can be clearly seen, and because man is something to look at that he can only be glimpsed. For, *firstly*, He can be — He must be — taken in totally at a glance, or not at all; whereas only partial views of a man can be had — side and front and back, near and far, inside and outside, in this light or that — one after another. Moreover, there is no end to them: it can never be claimed that the whole man has at last been observed. He will die before even his outside has been thoroughly inspected; as for his inside, it comprises worlds within worlds of hidden obscurity. Of the Self alone we have full inside information, and there is no outside to Him. *Secondly*, He is always here and therefore directly apprehended, without the distorting mediation of light waves or particles, eye lenses, retinae, nerve cells, and all the rest; whereas man is always over there, a remote inference who must in fact be quite different from what any outside observer makes of him. *Thirdly*, He is always now as well as here, coincident in time no less than space with His observer; whereas man is always then as well as there, parted in time no less than space from his observer. For a man is disclosed by light, which takes time to get from seen to seer: consequently the man that is *now* is forever and necessarily inscrutable, which is as good as saying he is a fiction. Here and now is no man, no thing whatever, but only Him who is mySelf and no thing.

In other words, it is my original face here, and not my human face over there in my shaving mirror, which is open to inspection. It is not that man's-head, but this no-head, which is real. "The perfection of vision is not seeing others, but oneself," says Chuang Tzu, "for a man who sees not himself, but others, takes not possession of himself." And among the others is that face in the mirror.

As the Christian schoolmen taught, only the Perfect Object can be perfectly known; we are necessarily more-or-less ignorant of all inferior things, and this ignorance is precisely the measure of their inferiority. Ramana Maharshi said the same thing: to know something other than oneSelf is incorrect knowledge. "Right mentation," Asvaghosa (lst c. A.D.) is reported as saying, "is the realisation of Mind itself, of its pure undifferentiated essence." This profound truth finds many expressions, as when it is said that the spiritual is capable of precise definition (T.R.V. Murti), or that God is absolutely simple (Eckhart), or that there is nothing inexplicable — or explicable — in Reality (Hui-k'e). Contrary to popular opinion, it is the mark of material things that they are dark and hidden and mysterious, whereas spiritual things are — once seen — sharp and plain and obvious. The incomparable Ruysbroeck puts it thus: "This simple unity is ever clear and manifest to the intellectual eyes when turned in upon the purity of the mind. It is a pure and serene air, lucent with divine light; and it is given to us to discover, fix, and contemplate eternal truth with purified and illuminated eyes... We are made free and void of every happening and every dream."

"The pure in heart shall see God" — for the pure heart is God. This, the only undistorted seeing, the only reliable knowledge — knowledge of the knower, seeing of the seer — is an understanding free from all imagery, a consciousness without content, a waking to full awareness by ceasing to be aware of any particular thing. In the words of Plotinus: "To real Being we go back, all that we have and are; to That we return as from That we came. Of what is there we have direct knowledge, not mere images or impressions; and to know without images is to be." This knowledge of ours is in fact not ours, but the knowledge which That has of Itself. As the *Bhagavadgita* teaches, the Self is Self-perceived. No mere man ever saw such a thing. The contentless Real can only be viewed at its own highest level, by the Real. It does not exist for others, who are in no condition or position to appreciate it: in fact, that is why they are unReal. "To comprehend and to understand God above all similitudes, such as He is in Himself, is to be God," — Ruysbroeck, though a Christian, dares to say it.

Here we come to the very heart of Mahayana Buddhism and of Zen — the doctrine of *prajna*, particularly as it appears in Hui-Neng and his followers. The Void which is the topic of this book, this Emptiness or Nothing which stands so magnificently alone, is certainly no mere Void, no common Emptiness, no negligible Nothingness: for it is conscious of itself as Void and Empty and Nothing. (This very statement is sufficient evidence of the fact!)* It is not only the Self-producing source and destroyer of all the world's richness, a fountain gushing infinite energies, and moreover the knower of Itself in these capacities; It is also the knower of Itself as at once absolutely knowable and unknowable, and neither of these — as absolutely free of all such complications.

For Absolute Vacuity to be fully alive to Itself as Absolute Vacuity, is no mean achievement on Its part! And certainly this astounding knack is no incidental accomplishment or divine by-product, but Its own very being. That is to say: Self-nature *is* Self-knowledge. Its awareness of Itself *is* Its existence. To be Itself, it knows Itself as Itself. Mere No-mind, unmindful of itself, is not the No-mind of Zen: the true No-mind or Mindlessness embraces its own awakening. Our enjoyment of our Self nature as empty is that empty Self-nature itself: in this act of insight we are what we see, the knower and the knowing are the known, subject and object and their interaction at last coincide and merge. That this absence of all content, or thoughtlessness (*wu-nien*), can nevertheless think itself is not only an absolute mystery: it is also simple clarity itself. It is perfectly straightforward, and complex and difficult only when we start thinking about it. In fact, no cogitation, not even meditation,

*After all, the Void is the Author of this sentence: it doesn't come out of my head over there, but my no-head here.

can enter here*, where thinker and thought are indistinguishable: no views are obtainable, all ideas are infinitely wide of the mark, where Reality shines by Itself, all alone, utterly unobstructed, unfathomably positive, *here*.

---

*Cf. *The Tibetan Book of the Great Liberation*, p. 222: "There being no thing upon which to meditate, no meditation is there whatsoever... Without meditating, look into the True State, wherein self-cognition, self-knowledge, self-illumination shine resplendently. These, so shining, are called the Bodhisattvic Mind."

Cf. Ruysbroeck: "Thus we receive in idleness of spirit the Incomprehensible Light, enfolding us and penetrating us. And this Light is nothing else but an infinite gazing and seeing. We behold that which we are, and we are that which we behold."

Circle in point, blossom in seedling lies;
Those who seek God within the world are wise.

Angelus Silesius

Shakti, see all space as if already absorbed in your
own head in the brilliance.
Waking, sleeping, dreaming, know you as light.

Ancient Indian Scripture, recorded by Paul Reps

Heaven is not in the wide blue sky, but in the place
where the body is made in the house of the creative.
It is as if, in the middle of one's being,
there were a non-being.
And the deeper secret within the secret:
The land that is nowhere,
that is the true home.

The Secret of the Golden Flower

Once between my folding hands I held it,
held your face on which the moonlight fell.
Thing, beneath the tears that over-welled it,
of all things least comprehensible.

Rainer Maria Rilke

Chapter 2

The Centre And Its Regions

I have, then, to turn about, direct my attention inwards, and keep issuing the stern command: LOOK WHO'S HERE! What then appears is this headless Wonder, this Self-portrait of a Nobody, curiously framed in an assortment of loose arms and legs. John Donne, exploring the same little-known region, made a similar discovery:

> Thou art too narrow, wretch, to comprehend
> Even thy selfe: yea though thou wouldst but bend
> To know thy body.

But he took what he found to be an unhappy accident, a defect of the human condition, instead of what it really is: an ever-open vista leading to the infinite depths of our nature. He lacked what we all need, a habit of radical empiricism, of childlike humility before the facts, however strange or disturbing they may appear. Shedding all preconceptions and preferences, we have to admit our proper place and real shape, clearly distinguishing the human periphery from the nonhuman core. Nothing more nor less than the bare truth will set us free. Absolute honesty with ourselves, the starkest realism, is the only piety that is any good in the end. "What does God ask of us," writes the Jesuit father John Nicholas Grou, "when He commands us to annihilate ourselves and to renounce ourselves? He asks of us to do ourselves justice, to put ourselves in our proper place and to acknowledge ourselves for what we really are." And this ceasing to humbug ourselves turns out, as it happens, to be rewarding indeed. As Grou remarks, "the practice is infinitely sweeter than we think for."

I must know my proper place and firmly put myself in it. It is the only safe place, anyway. The only escape route from all the ills that flesh is heir to is an inward route, from the place of mortal man out there to the place of immortal Spirit right here. Like Alice losing the Red Queen by walking towards her, or the ship sheltering from the typhoon by staying at its centre, or the cockroach evading the tortoise by taking refuge in its pursuer's shell, I must cease running away from my trouble and make for the very root of it: then it is — quite literally — cleared up. I am safe home in mySelf, invulnerable, invisible to every enemy. The *Dhammapada* says of the man who undertakes this inward journey: "Knowing that this body is like froth, knowing that it is of the nature of a mirage, breaking the flowery shafts of Mara, he will go where the king of death will not see him."

His journey to this central haven, though not an easy one, is short enough: a yard or two sees him home. "Let us flee, then, to the beloved Fatherland," Plotinus urges. "Withdraw into yourself and look... When you find yourself wholly true to your essential nature, wholly that only veritable Light which is not measured by space... you are become very vision. Call up your confidence, strike forward a step — you need a guide no longer — and *see*." And this movement inward, as Plotinus himself observes, "is not a journey for the feet". Rather it is a journey *from* the feet — from my human extremities yonder (where I clearly perceive them to belong) to their non-human Owner here at their centre.

It is a basic teaching of Plato and the Platonists that the corruptible body must be distinguished and held at a distance from the incorruptible (and therefore immortal) Soul. "Does not purification consist in the separation of the Soul as far as possible from the body, and the dwelling in its own place alone both now and

---

No doubt Plotinus, and other writers quoted in this book, often use the language of 'physical' space and of 'natural' vision metaphorically, for want of a better, to describe their 'spiritual' counterparts. All the evidence seems to me to be against this typically Western bifurcation of reality. Surely it is the gratuitous and confusing invention of a piety that has not yet fully faced the facts, which are 'natural-spiritual' throughout: indeed there is nothing like a 'spiritual' smoke-screen for taking cover from the concrete Reality that shines before our very

hereafter — the release of the Soul from the chains of the body?" Commenting upon this passage of Plato's, Plotinus writes: "What is meant by the purification of the Soul is simply to allow it to be alone... Separation is the condition of a Soul no longer entering the body to lie at its mercy; it is to stand as a light set in the midst of trouble but unperturbed through it all." Elsewhere he says: "In us the individual, viewed as body, is far from Reality; by Soul, which especially constitutes our being, we participate in Reality."

To our modern ears this teaching sounds vague and remote, as well as unhealthily puritanical. In fact, it is the reverse. As we have seen, the Soul — or Spirit or Self or Void — as ever-central to me, as always here and now, is necessarily alone, pure, incorruptible and self-luminous; while the body, as ever-peripheral to me, as always not-here and not-now, is necessarily mixed up with other things, impure, corruptible. and opaque. Outside authority for this statement — from the East or the West — is really quite superfluous: the evidence is never absent. I don't need to look up from this writing hand to see, more clearly than my hand itself, that this Self "is bodiless among the embodied" (as the *Katha Upanisad* puts it), free from all changing circumstance, an invulnerable stronghold which no creature can approach, much less invade. Another *Upanisad*, the *Chandogya*, has this to say: —

"Self stays in the heart; 'heart', a word that seems to say 'here it is'. Who knows this, daily enjoys the Kingdom of Heaven. A wise

---

eyes, all ready to enlighten us. When we try to describe 'spiritual' things, however, the language of things in space is forced upon us, so that we are likely to speak truer than we know: fortunately, our down-to-earth vocabulary does not help us to evade this world. The power of Zen lies in its outright rejection of otherworldliness; and Chinese habits of thought, refusing to separate man from the universe and mind from matter, certainly helped here.

Man, leaving his body, joins that flame; is one with his own nature.

"Self is the wall which keeps the creatures from breaking in. Day and night do not go near Him, nor age, nor death, nor grief, nor good, nor evil. Sin turns away from Him; for Spirit knows no sin.

"Self is the bridge. When a man crosses that bridge, if blind, he shall see; if sick, he shall be well; if unhappy, he shall be happy. When he crosses that bridge, though it be night, it shall be day; for heaven is shining always."

To find out what in practice this splendid Indian scripture means, I have only to stop all vain imaginings and look — look, for example, at the distance which apparently separates me from these limbs of mine. This is none other than the yard-long bridge leading from death to eternal life, from every kind of evil and suffering to unsullied perfection. This is the bridge I must cross now at all costs, from the dying body I see so clearly at that end to the immortal Self I see so clearly at this end. It is also the bridge I never need cross and never can cross, because I have never for a moment left this end of it.

Another ancient Hindu picture of our condition is the charming parable of the two birds. These two birds, who are dear friends, sit side by side on the branch of a tree, one of them busily pecking at the sweet fruit of the tree while the other looks on in silence. The first bird eventually tires of eating, and grows sad and confused. But when he notices his companion, who is in fact his glorious lord, his grief passes away.

As in most parables, the picture is perhaps more vivid than illuminating, but the practical lesson is plain. My suffering is at an end when, seeing clearly my dual nature, my two 'selves' — physically so close, in every other respect so remote from each other — I shift my centre of gravity from the lesser to the greater. Ordinarily, however, I am too busy with the fruit of the tree even to notice him.

Again, I am like a bird so closely caged that it imagines it is the cage which lives and sings and feeds on birdseed: the poor bird never gets around to looking inside the bars to see whether there is an inside, to say nothing of an insider with beautiful plumage and a sweet voice. Or I am like an oyster imprisoned in his shell, unable or unwilling to twist round and note that the shell isn't a uniform solid but actually contains a shellfish: he lives a shell's fictitious life outside himself, and never suspects that true life within, which enables him to live the fictitious one.

To bring the lesson right home, let me remind myself that the distance between the two birds on the bough, between the songbird and the bars of his cage, between the shellfish and his shell, is a physical one. It can actually be measured with a two-foot rule, as when I make my feet to be two yards off, my mirrored head a yard and a half, my hand one yard. Besides, this cage of limbs, this oyster-shell of mine, can be photographed; and though its Inhabitant, camera-shy, insists on keeping out of the picture, there is still to the perceptive eye a trace of Him in the extreme foreground.* If He does not figure there it is not because He is absent: on the contrary, it is because He is invariably present as the total foreground of every view. To the enlightened observer (that is, to Himself), He steals every picture, filling the entire foreground, and it is His face alone which is never blurred, or out of focus, or a poor likeness.

It may be objected that this picture of ourselves is hard to believe, that it turns the familiar world inside out, bewilders us with paradox, and offends our deeper instincts no less than our common sense.

In actual fact, the picture I have been trying to draw is the one we all really believe in, but are disinclined to admit, even to ourselves. It is the truly common-sense estimate of man. It is our universal, deep, unsophisticated self-knowledge, before it is vitiated by the things we learn at school and get out of books. However, though partially blinded (by a little science and too much imagination) to our real nature, we still have a working understanding of what it is. Let me give an instance or two of this profound, if scarcely respectable, wisdom.

---

*In early Buddhist iconography, the Buddha does not figure. He is merely indicated; for example, by footprints.

We don't believe in our insides. Each of us sees himself as empty, as a hollow man. The watch in my waistcoat pocket has works which I clearly envisage even if I never look inside the case, but the works that lie beneath my waistcoat I never envisage in practice, though I may confess to them in theory. Here, out of sight is out of mind, and out of mind is out of existence — out of existence and into the Void of my non-existence. One would have supposed that the thinker would spare a kindly thought for the infinitely complex world of brain cells he thinks with; that the eater would gratefully remember the fabulous interior universe which so obligingly turns every kind of food into the eater himself; that the acrobat or violinist or ballet dancer would occasionally enquire within concerning the mechanical marvels of his performance. So one might reasonably suppose. Actually, nothing of the sort happens. The man who wishes to know what is going on inside his car or television set, does not wish to know what is going on inside himself. He pretends — and practically believes — that nothing is going on here at all. Somehow he knows that he is neither a Solid, nor a Liquid, nor a Gas, but a Void.

In-short, this deep but unexpressed conviction of Hollowness is at once sober realism and (what is ultimately the same thing) genuine mystical insight, though as yet undeveloped. To be enlightened is always clearly to see two species of man — Solid and Hollow, Faced and Faceless, Regional and Central, That and This — and a world of difference between them. In practice, every infant and animal makes this distinction; and all our human education, which unavoidably is one vast conspiracy to unenlighten us by making us forget the distinction, can never quite do so.* Vaguely, we ordinary

---

*"How is it that this old man has the face of a child?" someone asks in *Chuang Chou*. "Because he has heard of the Tao," is the reply. Perhaps it is because the young child has not yet found his face, and the Sage has lost his, that to us their faces are likely to have something in common.

men do not feel like bodies; vividly, the Sage sees that he is no body. "I am disembodied!" cries Sankara. When a man is working at Zen, says the master Po Shan, and his mind and body vanish, he comes in the end to a state of "flexible hollowness". Another Zen master, Tieh Shan, describes the moment of his own enlightenment thus: "One day in meditation the word 'lacking' came into my mind, and suddenly I felt my body and mind open wide from the core of my marrow and bone, through and through. The feeling was as though old piled-up snow were suddenly melting away in the bright sunshine." His teacher comments: "O Tieh Shan, it has taken you several years to get here."

Tibetan Buddhism is particularly specific and detailed on the subject of "Visualizing the Physical Body as Vacuous". This is the title of one of the exercises, in which the disciple is expected to see himself as "internally altogether vacuous like the inside of an empty sheath, transparent and uncloudedly radiant, vacuous even to the finger-tips, like an empty tent of red silk, or like a filmy tube distended with breath."

Hollowness, again, is the central notion of Taoism. The Tao itself is hollow and limpid. It is seen in the still nave of the wheel, without which it could not turn; in the nothing a pot fits round, and which makes it a pot; in the empty space within the walls of a house, and the really useful part of it; and above all in the Sage himself, whose motto is "To become full, be hollow" or "What is most perfect seems to have something missing". This Hollowness is his indestructible wealth, his refuge, his immortality.* "If a man could only roam empty through life, who could hurt him?"

---

*This doctrine takes a debased form in the popular Taoist cult, persisting in China from ancient times down almost to the present day, of clearing out the body to make it incorruptible and so immortal. A diet of gold, or cinnabar, or jade, was supposed to rarefy and lighten the flesh. 'Eating air' also was practised for the same purpose.

Finally, there is a very early Indian scripture (recorded by Paul Reps) which includes these sayings:

"Suppose your passive form to be an empty room with walls of skin — empty.

"Focus on fire rising through your form from the toes up until the body becomes ashes but not you.

"In summer when you see the entire sky endlessly clear, enter such clarity."

With native wisdom, we all refuse to take seriously what we are told about our personal anatomy and physiology, our chemistry and physics. That sort of thing is useful for doctors to know about, and no doubt applies to other men, but somehow not to this man. Vaguely, we are all Tao-men at heart, hollowed out, eviscerated. For this vague impression to become clear seeing, we have only to turn our attention deliberately to this man and notice in what respects he differs from that actual man over there, in the tube train, in the street, in the lift. There is his nose, but where is mine? There are his eyes, but where are mine? There is his hat, but where is mine? Here am I, the only one who is in a position to say what is here and what is not here: and I say that there are no hats or eyes or noses in this place. Their absence from this place is so indescribably obvious that I should be ashamed to labour the point: the amazing thing is that it should be necessary to make the point at all. There is no concealment here: it is absolutely open and manifest that there is no head where I am, or brains or heart or liver or bowels, or tissues, or cells, or molecules, or atoms, or particles. They belong over there; this spot I keep perfectly clear and clean.

Nothing can touch me here, because every something is reduced to nothing by the time it gets here. To remain anything at all it must keep off, and be content to stay over there in my regions. It is true that over there, ringing this central Nothing, are ranged certain objects which I label 'mine' — 'my' limbs, 'my' hands and feet, and so on. But I do not always or necessarily label them thus. I can also, in the role of an amused outsider, watch them at their tricks, their swift and clever acrobatics. Often I detach these hands and watch them carrying on just the same, as of their own volition, with their own tasks (such as the writing of this sentence now), and then nothing remains to distinguish them radically from any other moving objects: and in any case they *are* detached — they are attached to Nothing here, and quite plainly loosed from any shoulders or trunk.* Again, I often notice these feet picking their own way along the path, and much admire how they avoid obstacles and maintain balance. I think of John Suckling's lines:

> Her feet beneath her petticoat
> Like little mice, stole in and out,

or perhaps of Tennyson's more direct experience:

> ...I touch'd my limbs, the limbs
> Were strange, not mine — and yet no shade of doubt
> But utter clearness...+

---

*There is a story, translated from the Sanskrit into Chinese in the 3rd century, which stresses our need to drop the thing we imagine to be here in the middle, connecting our limbs. An unhappy Brahmin went to the Buddha for help, carrying a gift of flowers in each hand. "Let go," the Buddha commanded, and the Brahmin dropped the flowers in his right hand. "Let go," repeated the Buddha, and the Brahmin dropped the flowers in his left hand. "Let go," said the Buddha for the third time, and the Brahmin stood nonplussed. "Let go of what is neither in your right hand nor your left, but in the middle." At these words, the Brahmin saw the light and went away happy and satisfied.

+Even the mescalin vision can include an experience of this kind. "My awareness of the transfigured outside world was no longer accompanied by an awareness of any physical organism," writes Mr Aldous Huxley in *The Doors of Perception*. "'I' was not the same as these arms and legs out there'."

It is only when I am clearly here that I am clearly not over there, and claim nothing for my own — whether limbs, or possessions, or persons. As soon as my attention slackens and wanders from this true Self at the centre, my false self is projected and attaches itself to face and hands and feet, to house and garden, to car and bank account, to relations and friends, and so on *ad infinitum*, with suffering to suit. Though the suffering seems real enough, it is all a dream, for I was never for an instant out there, or owned anything anywhere or anywhen. I am always at Home, living in absolute poverty, alone. Realising this, I can exclaim with Sankara: "I am without attachment and without limbs. I am sexless and indestructible. I am calm and endless. I am without stain and ancient." But the test of such a realisation may be a severe one. He is a poor man indeed of whom the *Sagarmati Sutra* says: "Even when his body is dismembered, he looks upon the phantom and image of his body as upon so much straw, a log, or a wall; arrives at the conviction that his body has the nature of an illusion, and contemplates his body as in reality being impermanent, fraught with suffering, *not his own*, and at peace — that is for him the Perfection of Wisdom."*

These two pink hands, which I take so very much for granted, deserve investigation. To their Observer here (who refuses to be their Owner), they are not inevitable, but only familiar. After all, it is an 'accident' that these five-pronged objects (one might almost say:

---

*There is a story (I cannot vouch for its truth) of a Buddhist monk who had attained to something like this perfect detachment from the body. Captured by a gang who proposed to kill him forthwith, he asked for one night's reprieve so that he could finish a vital meditation upon which he had been engaged. When the gang objected that he might, in fact, run away in the night, he picked up a large stone, coolly smashed his thigh-bone, and was allowed to finish his meditation.

these five-footed beasts, with long fat tails and no heads)* happen to appear so frequently on the scene. Their role is quite temporary. Their place may be taken — it *is* taken — by every kind of talon, hoof, paw, wing, pincer, feeler, and who knows what stranger appendages on other planets, in other constellations and galaxies. Throughout all the worlds there is only one Self, the One who is here. It is not another Self than this One who is now looking out upon a scorpion's pincers and barbed tail poised above them, and through a mantis's ferociously toothed forelegs, and down a crocodile's long nose and an elephant's trunk.

To Tennyson's profound line "Closer is He than breathing, and nearer than hands and feet," should really be added innumerable alternative readings, such as "nearer than claws and wings" and "nearer than leaves and twigs". For He, the real and only Self, is the Putter-forth of every limb, the Trunk on which all branches grow, "the stationary Principle" (as Plotinus puts it) "in the tree, in the animal, in the Soul, in the All." And He is also, as the totally Unconditioned, perfectly detached from every such embodiment — phantoms, all of them — and certainly in no danger of mistaking any particular set of struggling arms and legs for His own. Indeed, it is only because this divine Lodger is nowhere at home that He can make His home everywhere without distinction; it is only because He is wholly disembodied that He can wield every limb that ever grew.

Seiro has died; her soul has left her. Mumon comments: "If one

---

*I remember reading a horror story about a dead man's severed hand that comes to life. It escapes from its box and evades capture by running up the curtains and along the picture rail, before getting up to more sinister tricks. The singular fascination the story had for me may well have been due to an underlying truth. I really do perceive my hands to be loose, unconnected with me here, and busy with their own affairs: just as so many cigarette and beer advertisements picture them.

can distinguish what is real in this case, he will see that transmigration is like coming out of one shell and entering another, like putting up in one hotel after another. If he cannot see this, when the time comes for him to dissolve in death, he should be careful not to become confused like a crab dropped into boiling water and struggling with all its arms and legs. Now you cannot say that you have not been warned."

The essential task is for the Shellfish to distinguish itself from its shell, the Crab here from the confusion of limbs out there, the Songbird from his cage, the permanent Guest from his temporary hotel, the No-head from the mirrored head, and mySelf at this centre from everything peripheral — which is to say, everything. And then, when I am fully disarmed and pacified, when every particular human and nonhuman limb of mine has been amputated, all without distinction will be mine, and I shall be fully armed like the Hindu gods or the Bodhisattva Kwannon. Then, and then only, shall I be equipped for perfect action, with a body that is the entire cosmos.* Total withdrawal to this centre is the condition of total expansion from it.

One would think that this withdrawal, from the regions where one is not to the centre where one is, would be easy — not to say unnecessary. In fact, it is immensely difficult. Unable to bear the sight of my real nothingness here, I fasten on my unreal somethingness yonder. By a permanent stretch of the imagination (a stretch actually measurable in feet and inches) I place myself in my illusory regional wealth and absent myself from my genuine central poverty. Of course I gain nothing by this foolish manoeuvre, for plainly I can never escape from the Here-now to the There-then. But this does

---

*According to the *Gandavyuha Sutra*, Bodhisattvas can expand their bodies to the ends of the universe. Cf. *Zen Buddhism and Psychoanalysis*, pp. 61-2, where Suzuki describes the third and crucial step in the Zen-man's life: he no longer merely knows, but acts — with an infinity of limbs.

not in the least prevent me from trying it on all the time. To avoid evasion (how prone we are to take refuge in comforting generalities) let me give a very concrete and homely example.

Every morning, I 'become' the shaving man in the next bathroom. Just like Alice, I clamber through the looking glass, leaving my native country on this side of it for that very foreign country on the other. It costs me a mighty effort, a fierce tug every morning, to pull myself back here where I belong — and even then I catch myself slyly creeping back through the glass as soon as my attention relaxes. But I am really quite out of place there, and have no right of entry. For I pay no rates for that second bathroom; it never wants cleaning or warming; it uses no light or hot water; the architect forgot to draw it and the builder to charge for it: its clock goes backwards and the figures on the clock-face are the wrong way round. Though it is not an imaginary room it is indeed a strange one; it is wrong and will not do for me; it is not my property and I have never trespassed in it. In short, *I am not the man who shaves there daily*, and my frantic efforts to climb through the glass and merge with him are ridiculous. He is only a queer lodger, welcome to his own queer part of the house so long as he stays there. As for me, I intend to occupy the bathroom on this side of the mirror, where I perceive that I am neither a shaving man nor any man, but the Room in this room. I know my place. I know where I am now — not in that occupied bathroom but in this empty one.

If this story sounds whimsical, the fault is ours: it is because we live in a dream world that any glimpse of the real one must seem fantastic. In fact, the situation which the story records is so concrete that it can be accurately drawn or photographed. This is indeed no joking matter or contrived illustration, but something actually to be seen and strenuously lived every morning before breakfast. And if our house seems to be planned on different lines from the one I have described, and contains only one bathroom and no queer lodger, let us stop thinking about it and just watch. Then maybe one morning the queer lodger will suddenly turn up in his own second bathroom, while the first will be empty. That will be the day.

And if we suppose this matter to be one of intellectual rather than practical importance, let us consider these words of Ramana Maharshi on *How to Endure Grief*: "By turning the mind inwards one can overcome the worst of griefs. Grief is possible only when one thinks of himself as a body. If the form be transcended, he will know that the Self is eternal — that there is neither birth nor death; it is the body that is born and dies, not the Self; the body is a creation of the ego, which however is never perceived apart from a body; it is in fact indistinguishable from the body... The body is not real... If one thinks himself to have been born, he cannot escape the thought of death. Let him therefore question whether he was born at all. He will then find that the real Self is ever-existent and that the body is only a thought, — the first of all thoughts, the root of all mischief... You will recover your true nature as Unconditioned Life, if the idea 'I-am-the-body' dies."

Ramana Maharshi was perhaps the greatest of the modern Sages. One of the greatest of the ancient Sages, the author of the *Tao Te Ching*, has the same message for us: "The only reason that we suffer hurt is that we have bodies; if we had no bodies, how could we suffer?" But our task is not, somehow or other, to get rid of our bodies in order to avoid pain, but simply to realise our actual condition. As Meher Baba, another Indian master of our own time, points out: "If you think you are the body, you do not know your true nature. If you would look within and experience your own self in its true nature, you would realise that you are infinite and beyond all creation."*

Our looking glasses can bring right home to us these tremendous

*Meher Baba was specially interested in the so-called *Mad-Masts* who, like the Sufi *Majzubs*, are said to be totally unaware of their bodies. He opened a special ashram for them.

truths. Ordinarily, it is true, they do the very opposite, and fatally deceive us. Unlike the infant and the mature man, the immature man is taken in by his mirror: he sees *himself* in it.* The very young child and the mature man see a stranger, an outsider moving there behind the glass, but the mature man sees also the Insider motionless here in front of the glass, and observes the infinite discrepancy between them. And so the mirror, which started all the trouble, causing him to confuse his illusory self over there with his real Self here, in the end helps to cure it, by separating and placing them accurately. His nature is now perfectly conspicuous; it is because he sees so vividly what and where he is not, that he sees even more vividly what and where he is. By visibly putting off and removing to a distance the human mask, he discovers behind it his original face and eternally true likeness.

Narcissus fell in love with his own reflection in the water, plunged in, and was drowned. Every time we look in the mirror and fall for the face there, we repeat his folly and its consequences. The alternative is to look at the One who looks, to fall for our original face and its immaculate beauty, and then we are safe from death and every misfortune. That is to say, we have only consciously to stay here, secure on *this* side of every reflecting surface and every object whatever, in the place we could never leave anyhow.

I am forever this true and untroubled Self here, but I seem to be that false self over there, where I am bound to be in trouble. That is the trouble-spot, over yonder: and all my attempts to set it right are doomed. For there I am Self-alienated, beside mySelf, eccentric. The real trouble there is precisely that it is there, instead of here. My

---

*In Mr C.S. Lewis's *Perelandra*, this deception is well brought out; the Devil tempts the Woman with a mirror, and the Fall is represented as that ability to exist alongside of oneself, or together with oneself, which the mirror seems to give.

absence from here — or rather, the illusion of it — is suffering and sorrow. My so-called self-love is really infatuation with a phantom, with a ghostly stranger who is ever remote and inaccessible in his pain-filled world. Really it is absurd that I should be so dreadfully at his mercy, forever hoping and fearing for him, admiring and pitying him, constantly agitated about this fictional character. If only I could summon the courage to call this impostor's bluff, once and for all to expose this confidence trickster and his pretension to be something real — let alone my equal, let alone mySelf! If only I were thus to withdraw my favouritism, all my fond preference and special support from this humbug-self, he would collapse; he would be seen for what he is — merely one of the countless by-products of this unique all-creating Centre, deriving from It all his semblance of reality. Then, consciously where and what I am, my sufferings would be over.

In fact, this phantom self wears many faces, and is always changing shape. A disfigured face, a mangled limb, a burning house, a dying friend, a ruined business, an attack upon my country — however remote the wound may be from this Centre, the old eccentric habit is still at work: it is I who am injured, myself that is attacked. Just as I join the man behind the mirror, identifying myself with him, so I join these still remoter phantom bodies: I feel their hurts, suffer their indignities, tremble with their fears. And this inflated life of mine does not cease to be the ego's life, or less agonising, or less ignoble, than the narrower life I live as a mere man nearer home. Quite the contrary, I have taken the wrong direction altogether, moving out instead of in. I have only strayed still further from my Centre, become even more Self-alienated, eccentric, out of my Mind. My egotism does not cease to be egotism when it is blown up to national and supernational and cosmic proportions: in fact, it is all the more painful, damaging, and Self-defeating, and the haloes of public-spiritedness or patriotism only lend it an air of bogus sanctity.

No: the only way to end our suffering is to end the illusion that gives rise to it — not to get back here where we belong, but rather to cease imagining we have left this Centre where we are nothing, for its regions where we are something. Outer things have no existence there; what reality they can claim is Here at their Source and Centre, which they can never affect in the slightest degree. Seen thus as securely linked to their Point of Origin, their menace is gone; it was illusory anyway, and only arose out of their seeming independence.

Thus we are not required to give up anything, to behave in some odd way, to ignore anything out there, but only to put these things where they belong out there, and ourSelf where it belongs here. If we will consciously remain in our central emptiness, peripheral objects will fall away naturally: no effort to detach ourselves will be needed. In fact, they may seem to fall away rather too readily, as in the case of Lung Shu, as told in *Lieh-tzu*. Lung Shu went to his physician Wen Chih, and complained of a serious illness. He was quite indifferent to praise and blame, victory and defeat, riches and poverty, life and death. He looked at himself and other men, his own house and other houses, his own country and foreign countries, in exactly the same light. Consequently normal dealings with the people around him were impossible. He inquired of Wen Chih what illness this could be, and what art could cure it.

"Then Wen Chih ordered Lung Shu to stand with his back to the light. He himself stepped back and examined Lung Shu from a distance, facing the light. Finally he said:

'Hmm. I see your heart. The place an inch square is empty, you are almost a sage.'"

If we think this Taoist story — it is some 25 centuries old — to be merely symbolic of something, a humorously naive picture of some other-worldly state, then we miss the point of it altogether. The Emptiness is right here; and here it is far more vividly seen than anything over there. And no wonder: it is its own Seer.

We do not have to battle our way from our countless illusory selves out there to our one real Self here and the central Emptiness: gravity will see us Home. If we will let go, we shall naturally fall to the level which is our own anyway. "If you want to get at the unadulterated truth of egolessness," says Hakuin (who is the father of Rinzai Zen in Japan), "you must once and for all let go your hold and fall over the precipice, when you will arise again newly awakened and in full possession of the four virtues of eternity, bliss, freedom, and purity, which belong to the real ego." This is what happens when, letting go, you find your "mind and body wiped out of existence."

Falling inwards, diving through all the regions of our body-mind till we get to their Centre, we are totally abolished. For here and now, at this spaceless point and timeless moment, there is neither the time nor the room to build either a body or a mind, no chance at all to construct an ego. For these are essentially accumulations, patterns woven in space-time. They mean the appropriation and tenure of a particular volume, and the occupation of a particular address in space; equally they mean holding on to the past and reaching out to the future, and being present during a particular period of history. These unceasing activities are the very stuff of the ego or empirical self — of its mind and body — which is therefore confined to those outer regions where such things go on. Its home is necessarily out there, where it gets the room and the time it requires to build itself — by learning, developing habits, using language, remembering and anticipating, developing views and preferences and standing up for them. There is no rest from these immense labours; the ego is a process, the movements by which it constructs its own seeming solidity. Relaxation and detachment are death to it. Tension and pain are its very life.

Escape from this body-mind and its suffering is impossible in its own region, and by its own time-bedevilled methods of work, choice, taking thought, looking behind and ahead, desire to change the present situation. The Zen experience of satori could scarcely be secured by such means, seeing that they are the very disease of which it is the cure, or enjoyed in such a place, seeing that it has no place but the Centre. Here is No-mind, No-body, and No-ego — nothing whatever, and certainly nothing to be worked for or attained. Here alone is perfect health, integration, transparency, freedom, hospitality — not to be won, but realised as unavoidable fact, as *the* fact. Meditation upon this Centre is impossible, for it is meditation, it *is* Self-awareness; we do not concentrate thought upon it, for it is Self-concentration, and all our discursive thought about it is mere mind-wandering in outer regions where we shall never find it.

One day Manjusri stood outside the gate when Buddha called to him: "Manjusri, Manjusri, why do you not enter?"

"I do not see a thing outside the gate. Why should I enter?" Manjusri answered.

The Iron Flute

Chapter 3

The Empty Centre

To me, one of the profoundest and most delightful stories that has come to us from the East is the very ancient one of the Ten Fools. Having forded a dangerous river, these ten fools decided to make a count, in case any of their number had been swept away. To their great distress, they found one missing: however carefully each counted, he could make only nine. At this point a well-meaning monk arrived on the scene, and proceeded to calm them by an ingenious method. He ordered them to count the cries of "Oh!", while he hit each fool once smartly with a stick. This time they counted ten, were entirely reassured, and continued their journey.

In the regular version, that ends the story. My version, however, has a sequel. One of the fools was not convinced: he felt he had been tricked. He pointed out to the helpful monk that it was a question of a missing man, not a missing "Oh", and the recognised way of counting men was to count heads, not cries of pain; and so far as he could see there were still only nine men's heads, which meant nine men. And he began weeping and wringing his hands all over again.

The question is: who was the fool? *Was there a missing person?*

In case this tale should be dismissed too lightly, as oriental mysticism — not to say, mystification — let me supplement it with a tale that could not be more occidental or up-to-date: the perfectly true story of Mr. Godfrey's Morning Program.

Mr. Godfrey's T.V. commercial, featuring a typical American family, was uniquely successful. It was much more popular than its rival programs, and the explanation could not be found in superior actors, acting, script, or direction. Yet a panel of experts, including a psychoanalyst, an anthropologist, and a social psychologist, judged Mr. Godfrey to be "the most powerful salesman of our times." What was his secret? The panel found a very unexpected but very simple answer: *there was a person missing*. The Godfrey family was one short: it lacked a Mom. Automatically, the housewife-viewer filled the gap. In the ordinary, complete T.V. family she felt superfluous; in this one she felt indispensable.

No wonder she found Mr. Godfrey's Morning Program irresistible, without knowing why. Leaving aside all psychological subtleties, the simple reason for its success was that it was true to life, and its rival programs were not. It carried conviction because it was a realistic inside picture of a family, and families are always one short. Every family of X persons consists of X — 1 "fools"; and Mr. Godfrey, unlike the interfering monk, was sensible enough to be a "fool" too and not argue the point. He made his fortune.

I may gain more valuable rewards from a similar realism, a similar respect for honestly observed fact however foolish, and contempt for fancy however wise. "Make no mistake about this," St. Paul warns us, "if there is anyone among you who fancies himself wise — wise, I mean, by the standards of this passing age — he must become a fool to gain true wisdom. For the wisdom of this world is folly." It is a dream, fantasy, prejudice, pig-headedness, fear of the facts, exceedingly unpractical. Of course, it is clever enough: that's the trouble. True wisdom is naivety itself, and content to look *here* without scheming or contrivance. Maturity is only simplification.

Of mature Japanese Zen-men, Professor Durckheim writes: "The place these people occupy in space is in effect quite empty. There is nothing to 'go on', nothing tangible... They seem to be fully present and then to disappear into nothing." Like the disembodied whisky drinkers and cigarette smokers in the advertisements, like Mr. Godfrey's Mom, *they are missing persons*. So are we all. The difference is that they *see* it.

To such men, the clearest thing about the present scene is their own absence from it. Everything that is here, and comes here, is totally annihilated. In this, once more, they resemble very young children and many animals, for whom the disappearance of an object and its ceasing to exist mean the same thing. Out of sight is out of mind: out of mind is out of existence and into the void. The Zen masters have a summary and convenient way of disposing of an object: they turn their backs on it, or throw it behind them, or put it on their heads. Here it joins them at the Centre, where it shares their nothingness.*

"When Seppo (Hsueh-feng, 822-908) with all his monks was working on the farm, he happened to notice a snake. Lifting it up with a stick, the master called the attention of the whole gathering: 'Look, look!' He then slashed it in two with a knife. Gensha came forward, and picking up the dead snake threw it away behind him. He then went on working as if nothing had happened. Said Seppo: 'How brisk !'"

"Pack up your troubles in your old kit bag," sang the troops in the First World War, "and smile, smile, smile!" This self-administered advice was not quite as jejune as it sounds. I am void, and all that I put behind me, at my back, joins that void: it shares my non-existence here. Moreover there are no limits to the obstacles I can thus remove and dissolve — if only temporarily. With perfect ease I can take on board and make my own as much of the outer world as I wish for or need: I can make that body this body to any extent, because (seen from inside) all bodies are one and that one is empty.

Once more, I have only to attend to what is given now, ignoring all else — to stop thinking, and just look. Suppose, for example, I am standing alone in the bows of a ship and looking out over the sea. It is I, bodiless and boundless, who am racing over the water, breasting wind and wave. I feel as if I were the ship's figurehead minus the ship — and minus the figurehead. Truly, this is not a man at sea, or a ship at sea, or a man in a ship at sea, but a seafaring Void, in whose vortex man and ship and crew are all lost without

---

*The intuition that one abolishes an object by putting it behind oneself is very ancient and widespread. It appears frequently in both the Old and the New Testaments: God puts our sins behind his back, so wiping them out, and disposes of his enemies by showing them his back instead of his face. See *Isaiah* 38. 17, *Jeremiah* 18. 7. Jesus has a similar way of dealing with Satan, in *Matthew* 16. 23.

trace. This is what it really feels like standing here in the liner's prow, and what it really is.

No matter how huge and unseaworthy the vessel at my back, how drunken the captain and mutinous the crew, everything is in perfect order — once I, mySelf, take it on board. In this Place, everything imaginable is cleared up. I have only to take in and take over — to take upon mySelf — the most foreign of foreign bodies, for it to become this body which is no body but the Void. In fact, what I normally call "my body" is simply that portion of the universe which at the moment I happen to be good at dissolving, though all the rest is equally soluble, equally capable of incorporation and dissolution here. Just as this flesh, which is infinitely complex and opaque to my doctor outside it, is nevertheless transparently simple to me inside it, so this world, which is made up of insoluble problems as long as I wash my hands of them, is put to rights directly I make them mine. I am the solution to all my problems — and all problems are my problems. They can be cleared up nowhere but Here, at no time but Now, by no-one but mySelf.

Consider our own heavenly body, the Earth. Here indeed is a tangle of terrifying and baffling problems, all demanding urgent solution: the cold war, the arms race, over-population, race conflicts, persecution, suffering of every kind. This is not our heavenly body but our hellish body. And among its worst evils are our attempts to cure them. All history shows that, at its own level, there is no hope for the world.

Out there where I perceive Earth's innumerable ills occurring in time, they are incurable. Here where I absorb them, out of time, they are completely cured: they vanish into the Void that is without blemish, without self or substance or the slightest obstruction. In the ever-present Perfection which alone is real, they never existed. Here is proved true the Zen saying: "The Great Earth contains not a single dust-grain."

In so far as it leaves out any creature or thing, enlightenment is nothing of the sort. Certainly the Buddha's enlightenment, as described, for instance, in the *Buddhacarita* of Ashvaghosha, is no merely human or personal illumination: it is cosmic, and clears up all the problems of the universe. In the first watch of the night Gotama surveyed his own past lives and had compassion on all creatures; in the second, he looked "with the perfectly pure heavenly eye upon the entire world, which appeared to him as though reflected in a spotless mirror" and he found nothing substantial in it; in the third, "from the summit of the world downwards he could detect no self anywhere"; in the fourth, the Earth swayed as though drunken and became quiet and free from all evils, while the heavenly host rejoiced. According to Mahayana tradition, the Buddha saw his own enlightenment as the enlightenment of all sentient creatures, of all plants, of the soil, of Earth itself. In other words, the Void is indivisible: this bit of it is all of it. It is the universal Solvent: no problem is so difficult, no material aggregate so gross or vast, no selfhood so entrenched, that it can for an instant resist this infinitely drastic treatment — once it is applied here. The discovery of oneSelf as empty and marvellous is the discovery of all things as empty and marvellous.

Therefore it was no accident that, at the moment of his enlightenment, the Buddha was looking up at the sky, and saw the morning star. What really happens when, with an innocent eye and a truly open mind, absolutely unpreoccupied yet alert, we gaze at the heavens? Putting Earth and all terrestrial things behind us, we all merge here in a common emptiness which is our sidereal Void. It is no longer a case of "a hole where a head, or a human body, should have been", but of "a hole where a heavenly body should have been" — and even, in the end, of "a hole where a cosmos should have been". No wonder looking at the sky is wonderfully calming. This agonised planet is pacified in the only possible way: it is emptied, abolished. Its huge mass is etherealised in a flash; its seas dried up; its rocks wasted to nothing; its creatures disembodied. Here is the only real remedy for the bomb — a Bomb to end all bombs by blowing up absolutely everything. Not a dust-grain is left, but only this clear sky, Self-aware. Nothing could be plainer here and now than the abolition of this heavenly body. Just as the man looking out over the ocean became the ship and a seafaring void, so the man looking up at the sky becomes the Earth and a skyfaring void, yet fully and blissfully conscious of himSelf as such. There can be no peace on Earth but this — the peace of Earth when she sees herSelf as she is, egoless, utterly empty, and enlightened in us.

It is the bulk and weight and opacity of this heavenly body of ours, and the intricacy of its problems in time and space, which trick us into thinking that they are less soluble than those of our little human body. In fact, there is no real difference. Losing this eight-inch ball which is my head, and this eight-thousand-mile ball which is my planet, come to much the same thing: the one is no easier or more difficult than the other. For, truly speaking, there never was and never will be anything here to lose: the solidity, the suffering, the problems that we thought were here, are remote and illusory; and our enlightenment is not their dissipation but the realisation that there is nothing to be dissipated. Whatever I make my own here and now — whether it is this head or human body, this family or nation or race, this house or ship or plane, this planet or star or cosmos — in whatever role I temporarily cast mySelf, it is transparent through and through. I am nothing; I am the world; the world is nothing — nothing but this realisation.

Let me put the matter another way. Here am I, always at the Centre. As my real Self here, always remote and distinct from my false self or ego over there, I am the solution of all my problems. I am the true Elixir of Life, the Philosopher's Stone, the Panacea, the Medicine of Immortality. It is not that problems are apt to crop up out there — the out-thereness is the problem; it is not that they are soluble here — the here is the solution, and there is no other. No problem is soluble there, or insoluble here. And it is not

---

A more detailed discussion of "headlessness" at different levels can be found in my *Hierarchy of Heaven and Earth*; and, in particular, on pp. 112, 154, 188, 220, 224. My essay *The Universe Revalued*, in *Adventures of the Mind*, ii, may also be of use here.

a question of this Centre dealing with the periphery some day. The Centre is only now, as well as only here. At this precise moment (and there is no other) every knot there is untied here, every ugly situation there is beautifully cleared up here, every egotistical web is selflessly unwoven here, every dark spot there is lit up here, every mystery there is clarified here, every enemy there is pacified here, every tension there is relaxed here, every pain there is soothed here.

So it is no good running away from my problems. I have, rather, to run towards them, to face them, open myself to them, become them: and then they are solved. The only way to deal with trouble is to merge with it, because the real trouble is that it is not yet acknowledged to be mine: it is troublesome and menacing precisely because it is peripheral and not central, because it is there and then and that, instead of here and now and this. There is nothing so distant and hostile that I cannot subdue it by throwing over it the net of this wonderful Centre and drawing it to mySelf.

> He drew a circle that shut me out —
> Heretic, rebel, a thing to flout.
> But Love and I had the wit to win:
> We drew a circle that took him in!*

In the circle of this Self there is neither room nor time for trouble-Making, or trouble-makers, or anybody else — least of all myself.

The real trouble is that I am so often beside mySelf, so often not at Home. Everything is in order once I consciously move in, from that fringe of tumbledown outbuildings I can never own or inhabit to this magnificent Mansion which is mine for ever. To make mySelf thoroughly at Home, I have only to notice what it is like here — the unlimited accommodation, spotless and vacant; the absence of any occupant with his problems, ideas, memories, hopes; the ever-open door, through which the whole world can come and go as it pleases. Coming here, all its problems are cleared up; going, they arise again, but can never disturb the peace of this Place.

---

*Edwin Markham, American poet, b. 1852.

Chapter 4

The Great Mandala

All that I have written here, all that anybody has said on this ultimate subject, is metaphorically and literally beside the Point. Even the most sacred scriptures and the divinest thoughts are necessarily peripheral to this empty Centre, wide of this impenetrable target; and in this case the nearest miss is as good as a mile. Either this Point is seen directly, mindlessly, without words or image, by Itself alone, or else It is not seen at all.

For us, this vision is the most difficult yet the easiest thing in the world — difficult, because of all the imaginary obstacles we put up against it; easy, because even these obstacles cannot hide it for a moment, and nothing else is so plain. All we have to do is to stop doing anything and let what is right here shine forth. This costs us no effort and achieves nothing; on the contrary, our effort to lay hold of this Treasure is the very thing that hides it from us, who are that Treasure itself. When at last we see this, it is laughably obvious. There was nothing in the trick after all, and we are left astounded that we could have been taken in for an instant.

Reality is too easy to see, too evident: we cannot bear such transparency. Plainness and simplicity are the last things the religious man wants: he craves complication and obscurity, words by the million, intricate pictures, puzzles of every kind — something really hard to get his spiritual teeth into. He cannot bite onto the Void, but demands a substantial diet: food for thought, stimulants for the pious imagination, doctrinal pabulum to digest and assimilate — anything which promises to fill the bottomless Abyss and conceal him from himSelf.

Words and pictures cannot show us what we are. All the same, they cannot be dispensed with. In practice, and at all stages short of the Centre, we need maps of the country round about It, signposts to direct us, descriptions of the way in. Nor is this need mere perversity, or a superficial urge. It arises spontaneously from the depths of our minds, along with the pictures that express and satisfy it. Every country and age produces some version of the Great Mandala, which is nothing else than a diagram of the Centre and its regions.

Essentially, the Mandala pattern is simply a number of circles about a centre, like the ripples from a stone thrown in a pond. To these are commonly added squares in place of some of the circles, four radii at right angles, and all manner of pictorial embellishments. At the centre itself appears some specially significant or sacred symbol, such as the face of God, Christ, an Eye, a Buddha, Shiva and Shakti embracing, the Vajra or diamond-thunderbolt symbol, or simply a Point. The whole diagram is felt to be mysterious, holy, magically potent, metaphysically revealing, or just fascinating for no particular reason. It is found in all cultures, primitive and advanced, from the Palaeolithic onwards, and in the West as well as the East. In Tibetan Buddhism it reaches its greatest complexity, but Christianity can show some very elaborate examples. And its relevance ranges from the lowest to the highest human levels: from primitive magic and sorcery, through popular religion, to advanced mystical experience. In short, it is built in, a universal ingredient of our deeper nature.

In a more secular form, the Mandala now figures prominently in Jungian psychology, as the "unifying symbol" which a patient spontaneously produces from the depths of the psyche, when his cure is approaching completion. According to Jung, the superficial or conscious mind cannot reach down to the healing unity symbolised by the Mandala: and no wonder, seeing that it is only a part of ourselves and needs reuniting with our deeper mind, with the unconscious from whose abyss the Mandala emerges. The integrating effect of this emergence is said to be astonishing: with the powerful help of this self-produced device, the patient frees himself from emotional and conceptual confusion, and is as if reborn on a higher plane. Whatever its metaphysical significance may be (and the psychologist is not concerned with this) here at least is an autonomous psychological fact, an organ of the psyche which is as natural and as normal as any physical organ, and seemingly as important for our wholeness and health.

Undoubtedly this objectification of our deeper needs and processes, this spontaneous picturing of our hidden nature, works wonders. It would be strange if it were, all the same, misleading, more useful than true, and not much more than a convenient fiction. Certainly my own experience of the Mandala convinces me that it is, in fact, as valid metaphysically as it is valuable psychologically. This symbol works because there is nothing arbitrary about it. Indeed it is more than a symbol: it is as true a picture of what I really am as any picture could be. In some respects it is more revealing than any word-picture — which is not surprising, if in fact it brings up to the conscious and verbal level news of the underlying unconscious and pre-verbal levels. All this may become clearer if I now tell, as briefly as I can, the story of my own encounter with the Great Mandala.

My lifelong concern, and from the age of around 32 almost my only concern, has been the discovery of my own nature, the truth about myself. Setting aside all prejudice, all preconceived ideas, as far as I could, I kept putting the question: *What am I?* Confessing my total ignorance, and starting from scratch, I asked myself what this is here that I so complacently and unthinkingly label "myself" and "this" and "here" and "I" — just as if I knew all about it.

There seemed to be two sensible ways of trying to answer this question. First, I am what I am seen to be: I am the outsider's view in to this centre. Second, I am what I see myself to be: I am the insider's view out from this centre. And in both cases the answer took the form of a Mandala, a Centre encircled by regions.

First, the view in. My observer starts off in my human region, a few feet away, where he finds me to be a man — or rather, a part of a man. To get the whole picture — front and back and sides, above and below — he has to move around me, keeping his eye on this spot and keeping his distance from it. But clearly this superficial view is not enough; it is necessary to take a closer look at this thing to find out what it *really* is. So my observer (having equipped himself with the necessary scientific apparatus) approaches, through regions where the man is replaced by a mere head or limb or organ, by tissues, by a cell-group, by a solitary cell, by cell "organs", by molecules and still simpler particles, and finally by nothing at all. Right here, at the point of contact which is the Centre of all these regional appearances, he finds that they are not appearances of some reality, but just appearances. Clearly it is no good looking here for me, so he retraces his steps, passing through each of my regions in turn till he gets to the place where I am human again, a yard or two off. Now he reflects that of course I vanished when he approached me: his inward journey was my undoing, the progressive loss of all I need to make me what I am. To find the real me he must move in the opposite direction, taking in more and more till I am complete and self-contained, instead of less and less till I am abolished altogether. Accordingly he goes on retreating from this Centre, till he comes to a region where this man is replaced by this house, this suburb, this city, this land, this planet, this star, this galaxy, and finally by the empty sky, by nothing at all. To sum up, then, I comprise the Great Mandala itself — totally disappearing at its Centre and circumference, and putting in my varied appearances in the intervening regions.

So much for my travelling observer's view in. My view out is very similar. What is only here, is nothing: this Centre is visibly unoccupied. But ranged about it, region by region, are such objects as parts of men, men, houses, cities, planets, stars, galaxies, and again the empty sky — nothing at all. Thus the view out from this Centre, and the view in to it, confirm and complete each other. This is what I really am like, and the most convenient way of recording the discovery was to put it into the form of a Mandala.

But this was only a beginning. For the next eight years or so, this Mandala was the principal tool of my research into my own nature. For this purpose it took many forms (incorporating such distinctions as mind and body, past and present and future, incoming stimuli and outgoing action, interaction with other beings) and proved immensely suggestive as well as an invaluable aid to concentration. For instance, it provided a working model of this infinitely elastic spot called *Here*, which sometimes empties itself to a mere point at the centre, at other times takes in all things at the circumference, and at other times takes in some intermediate body. ("The Tathagata," — says the *Mahaparinirvana Sutra*, "divides his own body into innumerable bodies, and also restores an infinite number of bodies to one body. Now he becomes cities, villages, houses... now he has a large body, now he has a small body.") The centre of the Mandala stood for the all-devouring Void as it advances, reducing to its own nothingness here the contents of each region in turn; and equally for the all-creating Void as it retreats, producing them all again from this same nothingness. But the real value of this Mandala lay deeper: particularly at the beginning it opened a way to otherwise inaccessible levels. It exercised a quite irrational fascination, independent of all the verbal formulations which I have just described. Certainly it was no mere diagram thought up by the conscious mind to sum up a cosmology, to express an intellectual view of man in the universe, any more than it was a mere dream produced by the unconscious as part of an inner healing process. In fact, it was both of these at once, and valid metaphysically and psychologically in equal proportions.

And when this Mandala had fulfilled its function — when its conscious and less conscious work was done — it dropped away. The diagram that had held me spellbound for years was now seen as a child's toy. It was of no further use; for by means of it I had found the Centre here.

In my case, apparently, the Mandala had first to be formed out there, with its centre seen as standing for this Centre here but still remote from It, and pored over and cherished and worked upon as a thing apart, before it could come here and the outer symbol could coincide with the inner reality. It was as if I could become fully aware of my nature only by constructing an objective model of it, before taking up my true position at its Centre: the house cannot be built around the occupant — he moves in when it is ready.

If I no longer need this Mandala, it is because I have become it. At last, through its help, I clearly see my humanity removed from this Centre to its own region, a few feet away, where it belongs with other humans. Again, I clearly see every aspect of my infinitely elastic body-mind (ranging from the much-less-than-human to the much-more-than-human) in its own proper region near or far, leaving Centre and Circumference absolutely vacant. In short, I have found mySelf.

"Mankind," says Jung, "has never lacked powerful images to lend magic aid against the uncanny, living depths of the world and the psyche. The figures of the unconscious have always been expressed in protecting and healing images and thus expelled from the psyche into cosmic space." Of these beneficent images the Mandala is the most potent and universal. Indeed it is not to be despised, this wonderful gift to ourselves from ourSelf, this handy Self-portrait, this fascinating model or educative toy, from which we may learn more easily the difficult lesson of what we are. Let us take a few examples. First, a profoundly numinous nursery rhymes:

> This is the Key of the Kingdom:
> In that Kingdom is a city;
> In that city is a town;
> In that town there is a street;
> In that street there winds a lane;
> In that lane there is a yard;
> In that yard there is a house;
> In that house there waits a room;
> In that room an empty bed;

Jung finds it almost impossible to overstate the thoroughness with which these archetypal pictures (which are attributable to the collective unconscious) can change our lives and values, shifting the centre of gravity of the personality as it were from Earth to the Sun. See, for example, his *Modern Man in search of a Soul*, III.

And on that bed a basket —
A Basket of Sweet Flowers:
Of Flowers, of Flowers;
A Basket of Sweet Flowers.

In unpoetic language, my approaching observer, advancing through all my regional appearances, does not find the expected man: his bed is empty. Like us all, he is out, and has never been in. So the observer backs away:

Flowers in a Basket;
Basket on the bed;
Bed in the chamber;
Chamber in the house;
House in the weedy yard;
Yard in the winding lane;
Lane in the broad street;
Street in the high town;
Town in the city;
City in the Kingdom —
This is the Key of the Kingdom.
*Of the Kingdom this is the Key.**

Certainly we have here, in charming figurative language, the Key of the Kingdom of Heaven that is within us — the Kingdom that is smaller than the tiniest seed yet larger than the greatest of trees. The *Chandogya Upanisad* puts it like this: "In this town of Spirit, there is a little house shaped like a lotus, and in that house there is a little space. One should know what is there. What is there? Why is it so important? There is as much in that little space as there is in the whole world outside." In other words, each of us is a nest of boxes, with nothing in the last box — but that nothing contains

*There are a number of nursery rhymes which follow the same pattern: container within container, till we get to the Contained, the mysterious Centre.

the whole nest of boxes.

The Seer is one who, ceasing to imagine what he hopes or fears he may be, has the courage to look at what he is. After all, in so far as mystical experience is healthily genuine, it is only superior realism concerning our nature. No wonder, then, that mystics tend to make use of the Mandala — the symbol which is also a map. Tantric *kyilkhors* or meditation diagrams, the Golden Flower of the Taoists, the elaborate emanation systems of Neoplatonism, Dante's Mystic Rose, and St. Teresa's Interior Castle, are instances.

The last of these is particularly interesting. St. Teresa pictures the soul as formed of a single diamond or perfectly transparent crystal, but containing many mansions, with God's dwelling at the centre. Ordinarily, we live in the outer court, unhappily ignorant of what lies within. But when, by prayer and meditation, we turn our attention towards the centre, we find our interior castle to be immense. As we progress through its concentric mansions, a delicious sense of interior recollection comes over us; our breath seems to cease; we seem quite bodiless. At length we know a self-forgetfulness so complete that we seem not to exist at all: there remains only the empyrean heaven, a dazzling cloud of light, in the very centre of our souls.

No doubt the Saint intended this to be taken as a parable, a picture in space of spiritual things which are out of space. She and her nuns would scarcely have welcomed the suggestion that these concentric courtyards or mansions are located precisely out there in the regions where we are more or less human, and their centre is located precisely here at the spot where we cease to be anything at all, and Reality shines alone and unhindered. Nevertheless the Interior Castle is effective as a religious symbol because it is also (in spite of its designer's conscious intentions) a diagram of what we are in cold fact, visibly, in this very room and at this very moment. Whether we move into the next room, or go out for a walk, or shoot off to the Moon, we take this Castle with us everywhere. Its outer courts are always ranged about us over there, region by region, and we are always safe here at the bright Centre.

Certainly there are Christian mystics who seem clearly to locate and see this Centre, but it tends to assume a form (which, however sublime, is misplaced) and to remain other than the seer: the self and the Self do not yet coincide. For instance, the Lady Julian of Norwich writes: "Then I remained still, awake; and our Lord opened my ghostly eyes and shewed me my soul in the midst of my heart. I saw my soul as large as if it were a kingdom, and from what I saw therein, methought it was a worshipful city. In the midst of this City is seated our Lord, true God and true man — beautiful in person and tall of stature — the worshipful, highest Lord; and I saw Him in majesty covered with glory. He sits in the very centre of the soul, in peace and rest, and rules and cares for heaven and earth and all that is. The Manhood, with the Godhead, sits in rest, and the Godhead rules and directs without any instrument or busyness; and my soul is blessedfully possessed by the Godhead that is Sovereign Might, Sovereign Wisdom, Sovereign Goodness."

In the West, it is only an Eckhart who can speak of losing himself utterly in the formless Godhead. "When I go back into the ground, into the depths, into the well-spring of the Godhead, no one will ask me whence I came or whither I went. No one missed me."

It is when mysticism takes flight heavenwards, when spirit can find no place in nature, that the Mandala is most likely to arise from the unconscious as a partial compensation or corrective. Like the body, the psyche has its own means — entirely beyond our supervision — of healing its wounds.

But where nature and spirit are not so dangerously divided, as for example in Zen Buddhism, the Mandala is less likely to appear. This everyday world, these common objects before us — this cypress tree in the courtyard, this bundle of flax, this rice-bowl, this shadowy nose, and (above all) this original face — set the scene of enlightenment. In fact, it is our ceaseless attempt to escape from the ordinary and seek our good in the extraordinary, in some unlocated spiritual realm instead of right here and now, which prevents our enlightenment:

the whole secret of which is simply to attend to what is given in this very place at this very moment. "Stop thinking, stop evaluating, stop imagining, and just look!" say the Zen masters. "See what your face looks like at this moment." All their koans (or prescribed topics for meditation) are therefore secular and commonplace and indeed meaningless in themselves, so that they shall direct attention not to themselves, nor outwards to some other place, but inwards to this place which alone gives meaning to all things. In short, it is not that the man of Zen dispenses with the Great Mandala: he has become it. He makes his paradise wherever he stands.

Chapter 5

Epilogue: Where Do We Stand?

There is, I hope, nothing new in this book, nothing that has not been said by Lao-tzu, Huang Po, Sankara, Rumi, Eckhart, Hakuin, or Ramana Maharshi. If anything of my own has crept in, it should be ignored. On the other hand, the masters' essential doctrine is a living thing; and, like other living things, it survives only by remaking itself continually. It has to be discovered and interpreted all over again in each culture and generation, and above all by each of us individually. It has to be restated compellingly, in our own contemporary terms, if it is to come right home to us and live and be lived. This is the only position from which to see what the masters saw: if it isn't seen our way and at our address, uniquely, it won't be seen at all. This book fails unless it points away from its author and itself, and from the masters and all scriptures, to its Reader. It is about nothing else. In the end, only the Reader can answer his questions, because only he is their answer.

The sort of man who is likely to read this book is likely to agree that there are two sides to him, two natures — one human, the other "divine". He thinks of himself, on the one hand, as a mere man among millions, dreadfully limited, suffering, dying by inches, and more or less unreal; and, on the other hand, as absolute, free, happy, immortal, and altogether real. In every way, his human nature is the opposite of his Buddha-nature. Of course, many questions crop up (some of them important ones) concerning these two natures: the formulae and the disputes are endless. Let us leave these to the experts, and agree that the two natures can be distinguished. And let us further agree that the purpose of our life is somehow to shift centre from the one nature to the other. Our goal is consciously to become the glorious reality that we are, and consciously to cease being the miserable appearance that we are not.

To grant this, unfortunately, is not the same as to see it. At the most, we only half believe in our divine nature. If we really believed in it, if we really saw it, we should be overwhelmed. We should be bowled over at our own temerity, at the hugeness of our claim and its wild defiance of all common-sense. The man who wins the Pools in the morning doesn't forget it by the evening: again, it would surely make some difference to a man to learn that he was the lost heir to an empire. Yet we, who set up to be infinitely richer than millionaires and infinitely more exalted than kings (in fact, to be God almighty, or something of the sort) carry on much as usual. Our friends see few signs of our extraordinary good fortune: our enemies see none. As for ourselves, we have some difficulty in remembering to remember it from time to time. In short, it's quite obvious we don't take our claim too seriously, and mostly live as if we were only human, after all.

Not that we're content with this immense discrepancy between theory and practice, between what we try so hard to believe and what we actually believe. We don't want to go on like this till we die. We long for that other vision, for that superb Beauty which occasionally we glimpse. And so we take up a religion, study its literature, discipline ourselves, go in for meditation. Yet still we are stuck. We look around for a guru who will free us, and sometimes we think we have found him. But soon enough we are back to the old routine. In the end, we grow almost reconciled to spiritual failure — at any rate in this life. And then we begin thinking of another life...

If we are absolutely in earnest (and it's a big IF) Zen points a way straight out of this impasse. It is to turn from WHAT? to WHERE?, to stop asking *What am I?* for a while and start asking *Where am I? Where* am I divine? *Where* am I human?

The famous Three Gates, or three fundamental questions, of Zen master Ts'ung-yueh, boil down to *where is your self-nature?* As Dogen says, "Thoroughly to know the *abode* of the self — this is the crucial problem for all Buddhists." And, after all, this is only reasonable. If, in Paris, we wish to make the acquaintance of the Mona Lisa, we don't ask people *what* she's like, but *where* she is, so that we can go and see her: a minute's inspection is worth hours of description. Similarly, if only we will look in the right place for our divinity, our Buddha-nature, we shall see it as it is, and that is something nobody else can do for us. As for the whereabouts of this place, the masters are agreed. God, the Buddha-nature, the Kingdom, the Absolute, the Self, the One Mind, the clear Void, lie within, closer to us than we are to ourselves. Reality is nowhere but here.

But still there is a serious difficulty. "Some have never heard of the Self; some have heard but cannot find Him." And, the Katha Upanisad adds, rather dauntingly, "Who finds him is a world's wonder." Apparently we aren't so wonderful, for we miss Him. The reason is plain. Doubtless the Self is right here; but isn't this man right here too, and much easier to find?

In fact, he is not here. He is over there where he is observed to be, present to his friends (who are in a position to tell him what he's like), peering out of doorknobs and spoons and coffee-pots, lurking in cameras, staring out of that occupied bathroom into this empty one — in short, always hanging around this spot but never on it. This place is reserved for Another.

Now at last the site is cleared. Only the Buddha-nature, the Absolute, the Void, is here and now and real; everything else, including our manhood, is absent and visionary. Once we see *where* we are men, we see that we are really nothing of the kind. Having firmly put our false selves in their place out there, our real Self shines forth here alone, its brilliance and clarity unimpeded.

* * * * *

It is characteristic of this Place that it has no characteristics. Right here, I know nothing, for there is nothing here to know; want nothing, for no goods can be imported here; am nothing, for to be here is to be beyond being. Right here, I can never do or observe or think anything, or resemble or measure or weigh anything: for the time and the space and the motion, the colours and shapes, the weights and measures, are all over there. Only their featureless Origin, their absolutely uncontaminated Source, is here.

I don't *achieve* this non-knowing and desirelessness and non-being, this pure potentiality: I just see them *here*. Equally, I don't detach myself from worldly things: I just see them *there*, precisely where they turn up. Genuinely sour grapes, I couldn't get at them anyhow. The central Producer cannot mix with his regional products, the Light with its shadows.

The divine and the human are poles apart. No wide gulf separates them, but it is bridgeless. "Why callest thou me good?" Jesus asks. "There is none good but one, that is, God." We should indeed think soberly of ourselves, and know our lowly place. "The higher the ape goes the more he shows his tail." Any man who thinks he's God should study comparative anatomy and embryology, and if he still thinks he's divine, or enlightened, he should consult a psychiatrist. Without exception, man is wide of the Centre; he misses the Place of Enlightenment, the Buddha-seat, by a mere yard or two, yet absolutely. In brief, he's there, where no God can be. The atheist may well say there is no God, if only he would add: here is no man. God is nowhere but here, man nowhere but there. Thus we think infinitely too little of ourSelf, and a good deal too much of ourselves. Enlightenment is getting permanently cured of our central inferiority complex and our peripheral superiority complex. It is complete recovery from the illusion that we have ever been those remote phantoms called men, or living things, or anything at all but this immaculate Void.

There is bondage, misery, outer darkness, pain, sorrow, death. *Here* is freedom, happiness, light, peace, joy, immortality. I was never there. A man was there, but he was only a shadow. Enlightenment is finally ceasing to turn things inside out and upside down.* It is

*Some masters have actually suspended their disciples head-downwards over water, both as a discipline and to symbolise the overturning of the false self, which is held in sight of the still waters of the real Self.

allowing here to be here and there to be there. It is non-interference. It is the obvious in place of the conventional, the simple in place of the complex, the given in place of the imagined, the present in place of the absent. It is our coming at last to our senses, sobering up after a lifelong bout of drunkenness, seeing where we stand. For enlightenment, like London, is a place. Unlike London, it's a place we can't get away from; though this doesn't stop us City-dwellers, in our alcoholic stupor, imagining we are in Edinburgh buying Zen-tickets for the next London train. With the Upanisad, we plead:

> Lead me from the unreal to the real;
> Lead me from darkness to light;
> Lead me from death to immortality.

— noble and heart-felt words, but they amount to asking a London policeman the way to Here-now Place. Like Bunyan's muck-raker, we search, oh so carefully, in every direction but the right one. "There stood also one over his head with a celestial crown in his hand, and proffered him that crown for his muck-rake; but the man did neither look up nor regard, but raked to himself the straws, the small sticks, and the dust of the floor." Our pauper's hands are so busy out there in the rubbish and dirt that we altogether overlook our royal head, crowned with ineffable glory, here.

The infinite discrepancy between our two ends — one heavenly, the other hellish — passes quite unnoticed. But the fact remains that, however low our feet may sink, we are so tall our head — our no-head — is always in Heaven. Plotinus asks: "In what degree is disengagement from the body possible?" And answers: "Disengagement means simply that the soul withdraws to its own place." Actually, it never left that place, which is present Heaven, the Here-now. Rumi asks: "Wouldst thou see a dead man living, walking on the earth, like living men; yet his spirit dwells in Heaven?" And we answer: we would and we do, if we see ourselves truly.

One would have supposed the perennial state of the world left no doubt as to where Hell is, and Heaven is not; but we are determined not to know this. Though Heaven is plainly nowhere if not here, and Hell is plainly in full swing out there anyhow, we prefer to confuse and indeed reverse them. And truly, so long as we fearfully avert our gaze from this inner emptiness of ours, we see it (out of the corner of our eye) as a dark and even hellish void, an awful cavity to be concealed behind ever higher and thicker enclosing walls of "gracious living", behind screen after screen of clothes, cars, houses, property, reputation, money, and power. Our civilisation is a frantic and futile attempt to *make* Heaven where it can never be, instead of *finding* it where it always is. And so we talk of a "celestial" symphony, a "heavenly" garden, and even of a "divine" hair-do or bit of sex-play; whereas a vacant man, an empty head or heart, any inner vacuum, is always more or less infernal — Hell itself we picture as the Abyss, the Bottomless Pit whose terror is its sheer nothingness.

The result of this crazy mix-up, this attempted reversal of Heaven and Hell, is that, in fact, we find ourselves trapped between two Hells — the outer which is Hell because we try to see it as Heaven, and the inner which is Hell because we try not to see it at all. This is what comes of treating space as if it were all uniform and there, as if Here did not exist at all.

We have only to pluck up our courage and look in. It is indeed, as William Law says, "exceedingly good and beneficial to us to discover this dark, disordered fire in our soul; because when rightly known and rightly dealt with, it can as well be made the foundation of Heaven as of Hell." In fact, really to take up our abode here at the Centre would be to find Heaven not only here, but all about us. Viewed only from this Place, every place is Heaven too.

There are times when we are in Hell, and other times when Hell is in us. When we are low, humbled, depressed, made to feel small and empty, and we fight desperately to rise above this condition, then truly Hell lies within. But when this interior Hell is faced, clearly seen, accepted, and patiently attended to without protest, it is already half way to becoming Heaven. At last we give up the struggle and relax, consciously becoming this very emptiness which is gnawing at our heart: and behold, a wonderful transmutation! Fully seen and entered into, the aching void within turns out to be remedy for all our pain, the Great Void, Reality itself.

Suffering drives us to become what we are. It forces Self-knowledge upon us, and our misery is relieved. But we soon forget the lesson. Again and again our misplaced hopes revive — our false hopes in our false selves. Facing in instead of out, we wilfully overlook our voidness or nonentity, and of course Hell breaks out all over again. How tragically slow we are to learn by experience that there is only one experience — namely, experience of the Experiencer here and now — which is not, in the end, bitter experience!

CPSIA information can be obtained
at www.ICGtesting.com
Printed in the USA
LVHW021950210423
744932LV00012B/809